Dedication

To my children, Adrian and Wesley.

WHERE HISTORY MEETS POETRY

AFRICAN AMERICAN LEGENDS

WANDA POWE, PhD

Where History Meets Poetry, African American Legends

Historical details about the lives of each person inspired the writings of each unique poem by the author. Readers and history buffs are encouraged to learn more about these influential individuals. Library of Congress, Biography.com, History.com, Encyclopedia Britannica Editors, and Encyclopedia of World Biography Editors are excellent resources. The depiction of Rebecca Lee Crumpler was based on extensive research; however, according to the Library of Congress, some doubt this is Crumpler's "real" face, since no photos of her exist. Also, although there is no proof of the state in which Crumpler was born, based on information from other sources, we believe that she was born in Christiana, Delaware.

Where History Meets Poetry, African American Legends supports the National Social Studies Standards.

Illustrations by Graphexx.

Published in the United States by Diversified Solutions Pre-K12 Publishing.

First Edition
ISBN Paperback: 979-8-9853326-0-5
ISBN Hardcover: 979-8-9853326-1-2

Acknowledgements

Thanks to my father, the late Arthur James Powe, for leaving a remarkable legacy of perseverance and hard work.

Thanks to my mother, Reatha Mae Powe, for her selfless sacrifices, continued support and whose caring spirit lives in me.

Thanks to my twin sister, Dr. Rhonda Powe Coger, for the unique bond we continue to share and walking alongside me, as we simultaneously reached the highest level of educational attainment.

Thanks to my siblings for believing in me and understanding the true meaning of family ties:

Arletha, Deborah, Eric, Frederick, James, Jeffrey, Jerome, Marie, McArthur, Vickie, and my dearly departed sisters, Renee and Sandra.

Contents

Africa

Dear Africa
home of the mighty Nile.
A land that stretches
mile after mile.

Free to learn
to love to live.
Africans had so much
more to give.

Millions were taken
on ships in chains.
They suffered abuse
hardship and pains.

Slaves without freedom
and exempt from all rights.
They prayed for help
in the struggle to fight.

Thank you Africans
for refusing to fall.
You have change the course of history
that affects us all.

MARIAN ANDERSON

Contralto Opera Singer
Philadelphia, Pennsylvania
February 27, 1897 – April 8, 1993

"Everyone has a gift for something, even if it is the gift of being a good friend."

Sing Your Song

My parents had me one of three
and music was a part of me.
My time at church had been so long
to join the choir was never wrong.

A concert gave hundreds of dollars
to pay my way a music scholar.
Giuseppe was a good voice teacher
my talent was a major feature.

While in New York my time was set
the first black to sing at the Met.
Another time was to recall
my show was done at Carnegie Hall.

All over Europe my name was known
a time to reach my next milestone.
My concerts were for me to bring
I even sang before the King.

On Easter Sunday I was bound
to sing for those who were in town.
I could not do Constitution Hall
Lincoln Memorial was my call.

I went to see the inauguration
to sing the anthem for the nation.
The Medal of Freedom to succeed
when Lyndon Johnson took the lead.

A heart attack the death of me
age ninety-six year ninety-three.
My lifetime journey made me strong
Marian Anderson sing your song.

BENJAMIN BANNEKER

Mathematician, Astronomer
Ellicott's Mills, Maryland
November 9, 1731 – October 25, 1806

"The colour of the skin is in no way connected with strength of the mind or intellectual powers."

Reach for the Stars

My parents raised me on a farm
they owned the land out of the norm.
I went to school to read and write
as students we were black and white.

I taught myself and did not stop
my skills helped me invent a clock.
The loaner books gave me some tips
to help forecast my first eclipse.

A city had to then be made
the project it had been conveyed.
Then soon they came to me for help
to plan D.C. was a big step.

Two dollars pay was not enough
my race had made the deal too tough.
The first stone marker was installed
they did not mention me at all.

My almanac McHenry said
my skin was not based on my head.
My writing proved one of the best
my race did put me to the test.

Thomas Jefferson knew my view
hypocrisy was nothing new.
He did not seem to know the need
and would not take much time to heed.

Life on the farm was meant to keep
I took a rest then stayed asleep.
I learned about the planet Mars
Benjamin Banneker reach for the stars.

MARY MCCLEOD BETHUNE

Educator, Civil Rights Activist
Mayesville, South Carolina
July 10, 1875 – May 18, 1955

"Believe in yourself, learn, and never stop wanting to build a better world."

Stay in School

My parents chose to make it true
we worked the land and owned it too.
I was a child of seventeen
the only one the school had seen.

The children they had to be taught
a teaching job is what I sought.
My hospital and my training school
for nurses did provide the tools.

The Scotia Seminary was a start
then Moody did set me apart.
Bethune and Cookman were combined
the college was one of a kind.

Then Roosevelt gave me a share
Director of Negro Affairs.
The one female to represent
a member of Black Cabinet.

The Courier and The Chi Defender
I wrote for them as a contender.
I did my job as a part owner
at my resort down in Daytona.

United Negro College Fund
a founding member made me one.
My honor it was to proclaim
the National Women's Hall of Fame.

The first and only black of all
to have a statue in the Hall.
Yes reading is a basic tool
Mary McLeod Bethune stay in school.

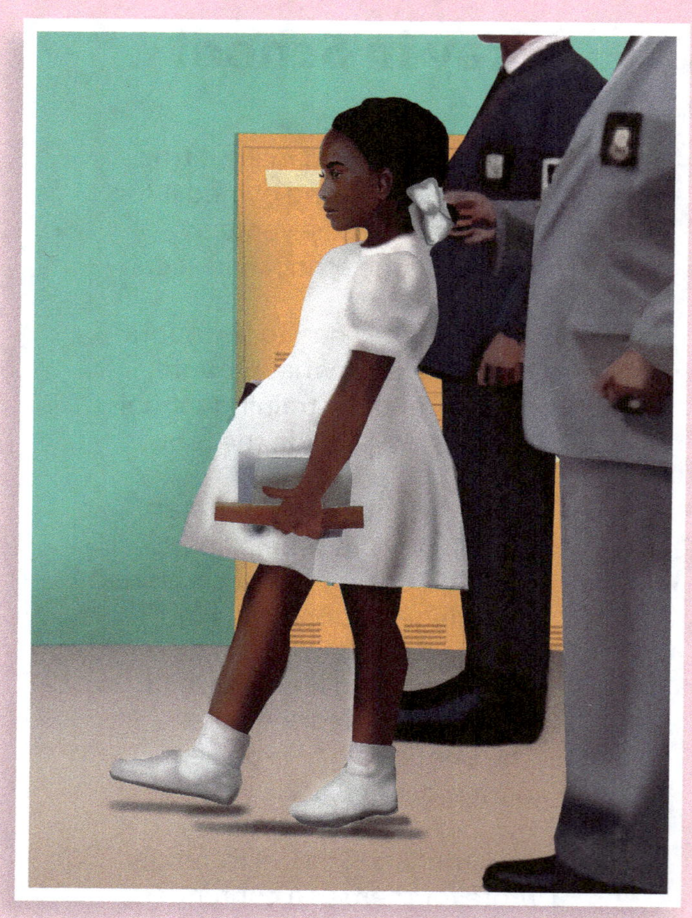

RUBY NELL BRIDGES

Civil Rights Activist
Tylertown, Mississippi
September 8, 1954 –

"Don't follow the path. Go where there is no path and begin the trail."

Dare to be Brave

We lived on a farm 'til I was four
my parents wanted to have more.
A better life was to be seen
we moved away to New Orleans.

In kindergarten I was smart
my work at school was done by heart.
I could not go to William Frantz
so then my parents took a stance.

The marshals did guide me to school
for me they had to change the rules.
My first day was spent in the office
the plan was to be very cautious.

The words were mean and very loud
to test my worth of being proud.
My teacher had taught me despite
she showed me how to read and write.

For one whole year we worked alone
to calm the crowd and ease the tone.
Then more black children came together
they made the setting so much better.

Norman Rockwell's painting style
told to the world my honest trial.
A book was done about my plight
and for the cause of Civil Rights.

I wrote my own book *Through My Eyes*
the message it was to apprise.
I did not fight nor rant or rave
Ruby Bridges dare to be brave.

GEORGE WASHINGTON CARVER

Scientist, Educator
Diamond Grove, Missouri
Unknown, 1863 – January 5, 1943

"Start where you are, with what you have. Make something of it and never be satisfied."

Farm the Land

My parents they had done no harm
we had been taken from the farm.
My owner got me back again
when slavery had come to an end.

My teacher taught me how to read
to help my chances to succeed.
I left for school ten miles away
my wish was for a better day.

Now Highland College took me in
my race had made them to rescind.
Ohio State gave me a start
a college of music and art.

As leader of the Ag Department
Tuskegee lent me my apartment.
Rotating crops was not an evil
to fight against the pest boll weevil.

To Roosevelt my work was nice
he came to me for my advice.
I made my goods with no tomatoes
but peanuts soy and sweet potatoes.

Then Truman sponsored too a bill
a shrine for me to this day still.
A postage stamp was made of me
for people of the world to see.

So many schools still bear my name
a U.S. vessel does the same.
I was called the peanut man
George Washington Carver farm the land.

ELIZABETH 'BESSIE' COLEMAN

Aviator
Atlanta, Texas
January 26, 1892 – April 30, 1926

"I made my mind up to try. I tried and was successful."

Claim Your Fame

Sharecropping made the job a must
my parents had thirteen of us.
At six years old I went to school
I walked four miles to pay my dues.

Chicago as the windy city
taught me about the nitty gritty.
I dreamed one day that I would fly
above the clouds up in the sky.

The flying school would not take me
to France is where I had to flee.
I learned my lessons overseas
then finished school and earned my keys.

To go back home I did remain
with pilot written behind my name.
My flying show had made me known
to all of those who had been shown.

In black theatres there I taught
my flying skills to those who sought.
I did not teach to separate crowds
and different gates were not allowed.

In Jacksonville I had to quit
my final show would soon be it.
While in the sky my plane went down
it shook and spun then hit the ground.

So many came to pay respect
a time of life to not forget.
The first black woman pilot named
Bessie Coleman claim your fame.

REBECCA LEE CRUMPLER, MD

Physician
Christiana, Delaware.
February 8, 1831 – March 9, 1895

"I early conceived a liking for, and sought every opportunity to relieve the suffering of others."

Take Time to Care

My parents' life was not conveyed
my auntie's home is where I stayed.
She took the time to help the sick
a doctor was my job to pick.

To Massachusetts as a nurse
back then my life could have been worse.
And though my work was not in vain
I needed time to have been trained.

I did achieve a med degree
from the NEFMC.
The first and only black to be
despite those who did not agree.

Virginia was the place to move
to help my patients' lives improve.
I had to give the needed care
to those who had no funds to spare.

To Boston I went there to live
my service was for me to give.
I lived on Joy Street Beacon Hill
a place to work and to fulfill.

My medical book without a doubt
it had two parts to learn about.
The volume also did embrace
afflictions of the human race.

My life had finally come to end
Hyde Park had been my home by then.
I had to do my own fair share
Dr. Rebecca Lee Crumpler take time to care.

FREDERICK DOUGLASS

Abolitionist
Talbot County, Maryland
February 1818 – February 20, 1895

"If there is no struggle, there is no progress."

Stick to the Plan

They took me from my mother's arm
to grandma then another farm.
At twelve they taught me how to read
and then I showed the slaves in need.

The harsh abuse it had to end
my master didn't hit me again.
My surname Bailey could not be
a new one was the best for me.

To find New York did change my life
with Anna who became my wife.
My second spouse was young and white
her race alone caused so much strife.

My message told about the ways
the dread of life those trying days.
I took my talk way overseas
once back at home I was set free.

My paper did go out afar
as slaves did track the northern star.
And freedom was more than a crave
my book it told of me a slave.

I knew just how to win the fight
I took a stand for women's rights.
Now Lincoln too heard my advice
for black troops who had paid the price.

With no consent I had not a clue
as running mate in seventy-two.
My faith was strongest as a man
Frederick Douglass stick to the plan.

WILLIAM EDWARD BURGHARDT 'W.E.B.' DU BOIS

Sociologist, Civil Rights Activist
Great Barrington, Maryland
February 23, 1868 – August 27, 1963

"It is today that our best work can be done and not some future day or future year."

Have a Great Debate

My father left us all alone
my mother took me on her own.
At Fisk University Tennessee
I went to school tuition-free.

The first black with a PhD
from Harvard University.
Suppression of the African Trade
it told about the efforts made.

Philadelphia Negro study case
urged one of ten to lead the race.
The Souls of Black Folk did profess
the thought of double consciousness.

Tuskegee was the place for me
I taught a term nineteen-o-three.
Booker T. had contentious views
Niagara Movement made the news.

The Crisis helped to spread the word
for many who had not been heard.
It spoke of what had to be told
a hundred thousand copies sold.

I kept the NAACP
then back to Atlanta University.
My fiction book was as a novel
Quest of the Silver Fleece a model.

The communist party is what I chose
I left for Ghana with my clothes.
My Encyclopedia had to wait
Dr. W.E.B. Du Bois have a great debate.

KAMALA DEVI HARRIS

Vice President of the United States
Oakland, California
October 20, 1964 –

"Our unity is our strength, and our diversity is our power."

Follow Your Dream

My Jamaican father like no other
was married to my Asian mother.
Divorce for them was to befall
we moved away to Montreal.

Howard then to Hastings College
a law degree improved my knowledge.
As a DA I did not slack
to launch the program Back on Track.

Alameda County DDA
my job was done a different way.
Bureau of Children's Justice deed
was done to help the kids in need.

California Attorney General came
the first black female with the name.
I opposed the law set by the state
to not defend Proposition 8.

My campaign work was of the norm
for criminal justice to reform.
The time had come to serve the Senate
the people they had put me in it.

In August on a certain date
Joe called me as his running mate.
A U.S. first was to present
a black female Vice President.

My books were written and stories told
my husband Doug *The Truths We Hold*.
Alpha Kappa Alpha we are team
Kamala Harris follow your dream.

ALONZO FRANKLIN HERNDON

Entrepreneur
Social Circle, Georgia
June 26, 1858 – July 21, 1927

"Some of us sit and wait for opportunity when it is always with us."

Own Your Share

My father owned us was a fact
with mother we lived in a shack.
Thirteenth Amendment set us free
I peddled for my family.

To Senoia by foot I was a man
I had to go and work my plan.
Work on the farm was not for long
the move to Jonesboro made me strong.

I was a barber with good style
and clients who came for quite a while.
Atlanta then was to perceive
three shops were built and named for me.

I had a business to invest
the Crystal Palace was the best.
With marble floors and chandeliers
out of the norm it was premier.

In real estate my money grew
my property sales had risen too.
Atlanta Life put me ahead
across six states my company spread.

National Negro Business League
a founding member meant to be.
Niagara Movement did proceed
I helped the local cause succeed.

The Herndon Home is nothing new
and still a site for all to view.
Atlanta's first black millionaire
Alonzo Herndon own your share.

JAMES MERCER LANGSTON HUGHES

Poet, Social Activist
Joplin, Missouri
February 1, 1902 – May 22, 1967

"...the only way to get a thing done is to start to do it, then keep on doing it, and finally you'll finish it..."

Just Write It Out

After I was born my father left
my mom to fend all by herself.
My grandma taught me as a guide
Ohio was home when she died.

Then words became my saving grace
in many books I found my place.
Sandburg and Whitman's poetry verse
showed me the way to be immersed.

Now Harlem was a renaissance
my poems in *The Crisis* had been launched.
At Lincoln U. some men and I
took the pledge for Omega Psi Phi.

The Weary Blues it would be first
the next one was a jazzy verse.
The Big Sea book it was so right
it told about my younger life.

A poetry teacher was for me
Atlanta University.
My open verse a *Dream Deferred*
was highly praised by those who heard.

I wrote many poems and plays and books
read *Little Ham* then take a look.
Then in due time my cash had grown
I bought with it a brand new home.

The Schomburg Center so renowned
my ashes lay beneath the ground.
I made my mark without a doubt
Langston Hughes just write it out.

MAE CAROL JEMISON

Physician, Astronaut
Decatur, Alabama
October 17, 1956 –

"Don't let anyone rob you of your imagination, your creativity, your curiosity."

Face Your Fear

My parents had to make the move
Chicago helped our lives improve.
Nichelle Grace Nichols on Star Trek
made me want to go to space next.

From Morgan Park in seventy-three
to Stanford University.
Cornell the school was next for me
a medical doctor came to be.

The NASA program my admission
a special job the main commission.
Endeavor flew up on the double
away we went up in the shuttle.

My business then was fresh and new
as one main thing I had to do.
The Jemison Group did make the range
for science and tech and social change.

At Dartmouth College I did teach
my students were for me to reach.
A school was built and named for me
a high school college academy.

I gave my time to organizations
like the World Sickle Cell Foundation.
My book was out and many sold
the facts for children to behold.

The first black woman of my race
to travel into outer space.
Gamma Sigma Gamma Woman of the Year
Dr. Mae C. Jemison face your fear.

SCOTT JOPLIN

Composer, Musician
Texarkana, Texas
Unknown, 1868 – April 1, 1917

"When I'm dead twenty-five years, people are going to begin to recognize me."

Go Ahead and Shine

My father was a former slave
My mother as a maid she gave.
My studies done at Lincoln High
gave me the knowledge to apply.

And Julius Weiss a German man
he taught me how to use my hands.
Piano was the thing for me
then Ragtime it became to be.

My opera songs were truly taken
no one to blame I felt forsaken.
A Guest of Honor did present
Booker T. with the President.

The Strenuous Life was so heartfelt
to honor President Roosevelt.
My many works and *Ragtime Dance*
were surely not a game of chance.

My time to fail had come about
I had to sort my money out.
Treemonisha now had been exposed
the opera show was most composed.

My publishing company not for long
I made new rags and many songs.
The Entertainer had a swing
used in the motion picture *Sting*.

For my disease was no solution
my death was at an institution.
I was called the King of Ragtime
Scott Joplin go ahead and shine.

MARTIN LUTHER KING, JR.

Baptist Minister, Civil Rights Activist
Atlanta, Georgia
January 15, 1929 – April 4, 1968

"The ultimate measure of a man is not where he stands in moments of comfort and convenience, but where he stands at times of challenge and controversy."

Stick with Love

My parents' middle class was fine
to serve the people would be mine.
To Morehouse College age fifteen
I studied text I had not seen.

To Crozer it was meant to be
my call was to the ministry.
I was a scholar PhD
at Boston University.

Coretta Scott she did agree
we took our vows in fifty-three.
To raise four kids was to achieve
as pastor I sought to believe.

The court had ruled about the bus
Montgomery Boycott won for us.
As SCLC President
for justice was the main intent.

My father had preceded me
at Ebenezer Church was key.
We had to protest segregation
I went to jail before the nation.

The March on Washington did implore
I Have a Dream was to go for.
The Nobel Prize and Hall of Fame
to this day still both bear my name.

The Loraine Hotel Tennessee
where James Earl Ray did murder me.
Alpha Phi Alpha from above
Dr. Martin Luther King, Jr. stick with love.

JOHN ROBERT LEWIS

Civil Rights Activist, Politician
Troy, Alabama
February 21, 1940 – July 17, 2020

"Nothing can stop the power of a committed and determined people to make a difference in our society."

Make Sure It's Good

A country town where I was born
to tenant farmers of the norm.
I joined the fight to do my thing
along with Martin Luther King.

The Baptist Seminary Tennessee
taught peaceful ways to disagree.
A sit-in landed me in jail
the Freedom Ride was more to tell.

The voting act had not been law
we lead the march so many saw.
To cross the bridge no turning back
a Bloody Sunday cruel attack.

My work was done to help minority
and voting was a top priority.
To congress I had made the win
Fifth District Georgia to defend.

The Medal of Freedom was an honor
from the President Barack Obama.
Shelby County v. Holder was a dart
just like a dagger through the heart.

The sit-in was no act of silence
in Florida to fight the gun violence.
My book *Carry On* did tell the story
before I took my place in glory.

The Conscience of Congress to bewail
on a navy ship my name will sail.
Let trouble be now understood
John Robert Lewis make sure it's good.

NELSON ROLIHLAHLA MANDELA

President of South Africa
Mvezo, South Africa
July 18, 1918 – December 5, 2013

"Everyone can rise above their circumstances and achieve success if they are dedicated to and passionate about what they do."

Stay in the Fight

I grew to be a noble man
from parents of Madiba clan.
My first name could not be the same
my teacher gave an English name.

When I was twelve my father died
no time to waste I had a guide.
Then I was sent to *The Great Place*
the people there they showed me grace.

A protest student of Fort Hare
I had to be expelled from there.
I did not plan to have a wife
Johannesburg gave me new life.

I chose to join the ANC
we followed youth league policy.
For Civil Rights we were deprived
through segregation we survived.

I had to face a treason trial
to be acquitted took a while.
Rivonia case for sabotage
a lifetime at a prison lodge.

de Klerk he let me to go free
he got the Nobel Prize with me.
For justice we had to decide
to put an end to Apartheid.

South Africa the place in fact
as President first to be black.
To stand for justice is your right
Nelson Mandela stay in the fight.

THURGOOD MARSHALL

United States Supreme Court Justice
Baltimore, Maryland
July 2, 1908 – January 24, 1993

"Where you see wrong or inequality or injustice, speak out, because this is your country."

Know Your Rights

My father's job was as a porter
my mom a teacher and supporter.
Court cases were more than a fable
we argued at the dinner table.

At Lincoln U. I had a life
I studied hard and found a wife.
Then Howard U. was done before
I went to work in Baltimore.

University of Maryland it was sued
for a black man they would not include.
We won the case with much attention
and in no time my name was mentioned.

NAACP trial was mine
I won court cases twenty-nine.
I helped black men made to confess
a murder put out by the press.

Plessy v. Ferguson sparked a sequel
to hold a verdict separate but equal.
Linda Brown and the Fourteenth Amendment
Topeka School Board as the defendant.

The Supreme Court was a higher goal
the first black justice was my role.
Allen Bakke was a main attraction
Civil Rights and Affirmative Action.

The movie *Marshall* a must see
with Chadwick Boseman starring me.
Racial justice was the fight
Thurgood Marshall know your rights.

BARACK HUSSEIN OBAMA II

44th President of the United States
Honolulu, Hawaii
August 4, 1961 –

*"You can't let your failures define you.
You have to let your failures teach you."*

Oh Yes You Can

My father was a Kenyan man
my mother white her name was Ann.
Then after they chose to divorce
Hawaii was still home of course.

Political Science B.A. Degree
Columbia University.
To Harvard Law School I applied
I earned a law degree with pride.

Michelle the woman of my life
then one day she became my wife.
For Civil Rights I worked on cases
to help improve substandard places.

Dreams from My Father told firsthand
my other book *A Promised Land*.
Two-thousand-five I joined the Senate
the time had come to put me in it.

Two-thousand-nine was to present
the first black U.S. President.
My second term I did not teeter
we put to end al-Qaeda leader.

The nuclear program was revealed
and six world powers joined the deal.
The Paris Agreement was so priceless
to help resolve the climate crisis.

American people I believed in you
to help us do what we had to do.
Affordable Care Act was a plan
Barack Obama oh yes you can.

MICHELLE LAVAUGHN ROBINSON OBAMA

First Lady of the United States
Chicago, Illinois
January 17, 1964 –

"You don't have to be somebody different to be important. You're important in your own right."

Plead Your Case

My father's city work was done
my mother had the home to run.
At Whitney Young I met the rules
as gifted in a magnet school.

From Princeton then to Harvard Law
minority work is what I saw.
At Sidley Austin eighty-eight
I worked as an associate.

Corporate law was to be through
then public service was to do.
My training program got results
as leadership for young adults.

I was a wife and then a momma
First Lady with Barack Obama.
I took the time throughout the year
to do my work and volunteer.

Organic foods and healthy living
a veggie garden was so befitting.
My fitness program was the mission
Let's Move gave me another vision.

My book *Becoming* had been heard
a Grammy for Best Spoken Word.
My conversations did rely
the stories told on Spotify.

American Factory was profound
first film released by Higher Ground.
I stood for all with pride and grace
Michelle Obama plead your case.

ROSA LOUISE MCCAULEY PARKS

Civil Rights Activist
Tuskegee, Alabama
February 4, 1913 – October 24, 2005

"Stand for something or you will fall for anything."

Stay the Course

By age of two my life had changed
to grandma's house it was arranged.
Pine Level was a brand new place
that mom and I had to embrace.

To finish high school with my class
could not be done but came to pass.
To help promote the unity
I worked in the community.

December nineteen-forty-three
I joined the NAACP.
The fifties had been very cruel
still Jim Crow Laws and separate schools.

Though it was wrong to be confined
I rode the bus and sat assigned.
Then told to move was too a fact
it happened because I was black.

I did not go another place
the law was to suppress my race.
To jail I went to from my seat
I stood for justice not defeat.

They found me guilty during the trial
we shunned the bus for quite a while.
Martin Luther King and the MIA.
they led the protests day to day.

Supreme Court ruled that it was right
for us to sit anywhere despite.
The order was made to enforce
Rosa *Parks* stay the course.

JACKIE ROOSEVELT ROBINSON

Baseball Player
Cairo, Georgia
January 31, 1919 – October 24, 1972

"The right of every American to first-class citizenship is the most important issue of our time."

Be a Good Teammate

My parents had me one of five
my mother raised me to survive.
At Pasadena Junior College
I showed my skills and gained the knowledge.

UCLA had to report
my varsity wins for many sports.
Before my time I had to leave
I could not make it to achieve.

I took a chance to play football
but it was not much time at all.
The war began and I was in it
a U.S. Army Second Lieutenant.

To jail I went and that's a fact
'cause on the bus I didn't move back.
In the Negro League I did my part
for the Dodgers it was time to start.

At Ebbets Field the crowd was mean
and nasty words came from the team.
The National League and World Series
gave me no time to be at ease.

My long term goal was for good reasons
to boost my score across ten seasons.
I changed my role to call the plays
which took me to another phase.

For Civil Rights I made the claim
I'm in the Baseball Hall of Fame.
I hit the ball and touched home plate
Jackie Robinson be a good teammate.

ELIZABETH 'BESSIE' SMITH

Blues Singer
Chattanooga, Tennessee
April 15, 1894 – September 26, 1937

"Listen to my story and everything will come out true."

Sing the Blues

Before my teens my parents died
my aunt was there to be my guide.
I did my dances with the flow
while as a minstrel in the show.

I sang my song *Down Hearted Blues*
about some things nobody knew.
Columbia Records made it be
for Louis Armstrong to work with me.

Ma Rainey showed me how to aim
Empress of the Blues became my name.
The best performer of my day
I earned the fame and highest pay.

Nobody Knows When You're Down and Out
a popular song and hit no doubt.
The market crash came very soon
the money lost halted the boom.

The time it was the Great Depression
a famous life had been my lesson.
With hundreds of my records made
the many songs were often played.

The *Bessie* print in seventy-two
it told some things nobody knew.
Now *Bessie* and the Queen Latifah
it showed my life a soulful diva.

For sure I died in aching pain
it was in fact my race to blame.
The Hall of Fame made me the news
Bessie Smith sing the blues.

HARRIET TUBMAN

Abolitionist, Political Activist
Auburn, New York
Unknown, 1820–1825 – March 10, 1913

"You have the strength, the patience and the passion to reach for the stars and change the world."

Have Faith in You

My father had been reassigned
then I was born the fifth of nine.
I'd heard that I was next for sale
my song was meant to bid farewell.

The Underground Railroad paved the way
for the journeys we took day to day.
We chose to leave no turning back
we had to run and stay on track.

As Moses I had to bring forth
a way to get the slaves up north.
Despite the fear that came in waves
I never once did lose a slave.

The Fugitive Slave Law was a fact
to caught the slaves and send them back.
The Canada route defied the test
to stay the course while on the quest.

The Union Army was a try
back then my job was as a spy.
I had been tough and not afraid
to stand for those who needed aid.

Not long ago it was revealed
to place my picture on a bill.
The Biden team took on the case
to put me in A. Jackson's place.

I fought for freedom not for strife
to try to live a better life.
We had to pray for something new
Harriet Tubman have faith in you.

ISABELLA
'SOJOURNER TRUTH'
BAUMFREE

Abolitionist, Women's Rights Activist
Rifton, New York
Unknown, 1797 – November 26, 1883

"Truth is powerful and it prevails."

Endure the Plight

We lived a life as toiling slaves
to twelve of us my parents gave.
My childhood days were not to keep
they sold me with a flock of sheep.

My master and I did agree
that he would soon let me be free.
I had to leave with one in tow
the other children could not go.

Then soon one day we had been taken
Dumont thought he had been forsaken.
Van Wagenens paid him for the trade
to buy my freedom as a maid.

He sold my son I had to fight
I filed a suit Dumont was white.
Then soon enough I won the case
the first black woman of my race.

My Christian life was not the same
I had to preach and change my name.
Ain't I A Woman was my speech
for Women's Rights I had to teach.

I called black men to Civil War
like Harriet Tubman was for sure.
I rallied people for the need
to give to poor black refugees.

Now Lincoln heard my call for change
then to the White House was arranged.
I never learned to read or write
Sojourner Truth endure the plight.

SARAH
'MADAME C. J. WALKER'
BREEDLOVE

Entrepreneur, Philanthropist
Delta, Louisiana
December 23, 1867 – May 25, 1919

"Don't sit down and wait for the opportunities to come. Get up and make them."

Love Your Hair

We had to work to farm the land
the daily grind was done by hand.
First in my family born as free
the early years were hard for me.

When I was young my parents died
my sister's home was to reside.
To stop abuse I fled the scene
I found my husband at fourteen.

When Moses died we had to leave
Missouri was the place to be.
A dollar-fifty pay each day
was not enough to make a way.

We moved to Denver to get through
my products sold like new shampoo.
And then came Charles to change my name
I did my work and earned the fame.

In nineteen-ten my business moved
my profit needed to improve.
I chose my workers to mentor
they sold my goods from door to door.

My company had been tried and true
my agents did some training too.
My haircare was a great success
and known by many as the best.

I lived my life then on my own
to see my New York country home.
The first black woman millionaire
Madame C. J. Walker love your hair.

RAPHAEL GAMALIEL WARNOCK

United States Senator
Savannah, Georgia
July 23, 1969 –

*"Keep the faith. Keep your head up.
It's dark now, but the dawn is coming."*

You Can Win It

My parents chose to preach the gospel
to lead the people Pentecostal.
The program from the HUD Department
provided us with an apartment.

Atlanta Morehouse was for me
to learn and earn a PhD.
To lead the church not just a thing
but home of Martin Luther King.

I stood for people working age
to help them earn a better wage.
For healthcare plans and voting rights
I fought for them with all my might.

New Georgia Project was a goal
a chance to serve another role.
The year two-thousand-seventeen
I made a choice to join the team.

On agriculture I was heard
I did my best to spread the word.
Environmental justice was a start
with needed help we did our part.

I had to learn through trying times
to keep the faith and know the signs.
To serve at least the next two years
I hope my work would be revered.

I serve the church a Baptist minister.
and Georgia as a first black senator.
From the projects to the Senate
Reverend Raphael Warnock you can win it.

BOOKER TALIAFERRO WASHINGTON

Educator, Author
Tuskegee, Alabama
April 5, 1856 – November 14, 1915

"Associate yourself with people of good quality, for it is better to be alone than in bad company."

Share Your Story

My mother was a slave alone
also my father was unknown.
While on the farm I did not to flee
Post-Civil War we were set free.

The Institute as I was told
came from the men who mined the coal.
I took the walk five hundred miles
to Virginia with so many trials.

Now Armstrong called on me to teach
to lead the school was in my reach.
Tuskegee opened up its door
George Carver came and many more.

My message was a big surprise
known as *Atlanta Compromise.*
I told the blacks to then accept
the status quo a main precept.

My speech it caused so much complaining
for blacks to do vocation training.
For equal rights Du Bois commented
the Fourteenth was the sole amendment.

I paid the court to challenge cases
to bring together all the races.
I wrote my letters in a code
against the lynching episodes.

The first black one and of my kind
went to the White House and to dine.
Now *Up from Slavery* hope of glory
Booker T. Washington share your story.

PHILLIS WHEATLEY

Poet, Author
Senegambia, Africa
May 8, 1753 – December 5, 1784

"Imagination! Who can sing thy force?"

Write a Poem

I was kidnapped and afraid
then shipped to Boston for the trade.
John and Susanna took the lead
they showed me that I could succeed.

I learned to read and write as taught
to be a poet was not a thought.
Then English Latin and also Greek
is what I learned to write and speak.

At age thirteen my rhyme was printed
a tale at sea with two men in it.
Various Subjects Religious Morals
the first black female book of poems.

Washington got a poem from me
the Commander had the chance to see.
I took the time to visit him
at his request not on a whim.

My trip to London was for sure
to share my work and seek a cure.
Then back to Boston to reside
in time the Wheatley couple died.

My husband John and I were poor
with many struggles to endure.
And so I did put down my pen
my wish to write came to an end.

I wrote a poem *Liberty and Peace*
to mark the day the war did cease.
Somehow I made it through the storm
Phillis Wheatley write a poem.

OPRAH GAIL WINFREY

Talk Show Host, Television Network Owner
Kosciusko, Mississippi
January 29, 1954 –

"Do the one thing you think you cannot do. Fail at it. Try again. Do better the second time."

Show Your Flair

After I was born my parents split
my grandma's place had to be it.
I won the Miss Black Tennessee
then to the state's university.

As host I ran a morning chat
People Are Talking was for that.
Chicago was the place to go
a better chance to run my show.

Year eighty-six I earned the fame
a talk show after my own name.
I pledged to keep it scandal free.
HARPO Productions ABC

The Color Purple had been named
a nominee it was acclaimed.
Then to the project called *Beloved*
starring me and Danny Glover.

One day a month it could be seen
life and beauty *O Magazine.*
After many years my show was gone
it was time to do it on my *OWN*.

The Medal of Freedom was an honor
from the President Barack Obama.
The Golden Globes did recognize
a lifetime feat no compromise.

My *Leadership Academy*
will be my greatest legacy.
The first black woman billionaire
Oprah Winfrey share your flair.

About the Author

Early in life, Wanda Powe was influenced by her 8th grade English teacher's grace, poise and brilliance. As a result, the native of Meridian, Mississippi decided to become an educator.

Despite the challenges she faced throughout her younger years, Powe persevered in her efforts to achieve. She attributes her accomplishments to her close-knit family and those who selflessly gave of their time to provide support and guidance along the way.

Powe began her teaching career as an elementary school paraprofessional. After attaining a Bachelor of Science degree from Livingston University, now named the University of West Alabama, she eventually earned a PhD from Mississippi State University. After having served in various capacities, she became a school administrator.

Dr. Powe knows first-hand about the determination, support and encouragement that people, and especially children, need to stay the course against all odds. Her passion to write poetry has been inspired by her own stories of love, life and ordinary matters with the belief that the power of words can impact a lifetime of achievement. In fact, the compilation of rhyme presented in *Where History Meets Poetry, African American Legends* was inspired 25 years ago by her former secondary students at Marion Park Alternative Complex in Meridian.

Based in Atlanta, Georgia, Dr. Wanda Powe is the founder of the training company, Diversified Solutions PreK-12. Providing resources and support to both educators and students, including those with special needs, is her mission. As a longtime educator, Dr. Powe is a personal and professional growth specialist committed to the business of educating and empowering people to reach their greatest potential.

DiversifiedSolutionsPreK12.com

www.ingramcontent.com/pod-product-compliance
Lightning Source LLC
Chambersburg PA
CBHW050323010526
44119CB00003B/85

* 9 7 9 8 9 8 5 3 3 2 6 1 2 *